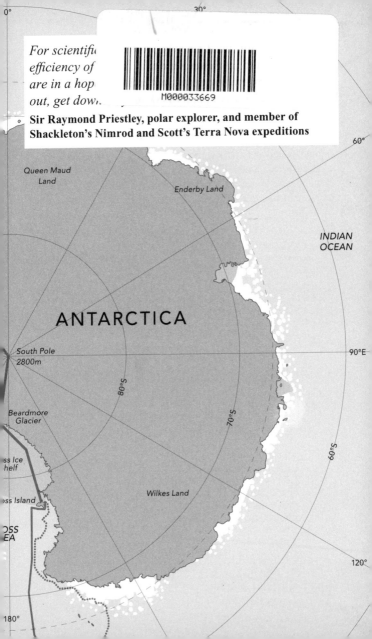

For scientifi[c] efficiency of are in a hop out, get dow[n]

Sir Raymond Priestley, polar explorer, and member of Shackleton's Nimrod and Scott's Terra Nova expeditions

Queen Maud Land

Enderby Land

INDIAN OCEAN

ANTARCTICA

South Pole 2800m

90°E

Beardmore Glacier

80°S

70°S

60°S

[R]ss Ice [S]helf

[R]ss Island

[R]OSS [S]EA

Wilkes Land

120°

180°

30°

0°

60°

Series 117

This is a Ladybird Expert book, one of a series of titles for an adult readership. Written by some of the leading lights and outstanding communicators in their fields and published by one of the most trusted and well-loved names in books, the Ladybird Expert series provides clear, accessible and authoritative introductions, informed by expert opinion, to key subjects drawn from science, history and culture.

Every effort has been made to ensure images are correctly attributed, however if any omission or error has been made please notify the Publisher for correction in future editions.

The publisher would like to thank the following for the illustrative references for the book:
Cover image created from photographic reference © Scott Polar Research Institute and © Getty Images; page 7 from photo © Bridgeman Images

MICHAEL JOSEPH

UK | USA | Canada | Ireland | Australia
India | New Zealand | South Africa

Michael Joseph is part of the Penguin Random House group of companies whose addresses can be found at global.penguinrandomhouse.com

 Penguin
Random House
UK

First published 2017
001

Text copyright © Ben Saunders, 2017

All images copyright © Ladybird Books Ltd, 2017

The moral right of the author has been asserted

Printed in Italy by L.E.G.O. S.p.A.

A CIP catalogue record for this book is available from the British Library
ISBN: 978–0–718–18727–9

www.greenpenguin.co.uk

Sir Ernest Shackleton

Ben Saunders

with illustrations by
Rowan Clifford

*Dedicated to Lt. Col. Henry Worsley, MBE
4 October 1960 – 24 January 2016*

Ladybird Books Ltd, London

Antarctica is the coldest, windiest, highest-altitude, driest continent on Earth. It is the same size as China and India combined, and most of this vast area is covered in an ice sheet more than a mile thick. The coldest ever temperature on Earth was recorded in Antarctica in the 1980s: −89.2°C.

Human exploration of the world's southernmost extreme started in the eighteenth century, when Captain James Cook and his crew first crossed the Antarctic Circle. For nearly fifty years afterwards there was speculation about a southern continent, Terra Australis, but land wasn't spotted until 1820.

In 1823, the English seal hunter James Weddell sailed 3 degrees further south than Cook, reaching 74 degrees south. The sea (and the type of seal indigenous to it) were both named after him, and no boat was able to penetrate the Weddell Sea again for eighty years.

Great Britain dispatched an expedition in 1839 to find the South Magnetic Pole, with two ships named *Erebus* and *Terror* under the command of Sir James Clark Ross. The naval officer and his crew went on to discover Victoria Land, the Ross Sea, Ross Island, Mount Erebus and the Ross Ice Shelf.

In 1901, another captain of the Royal Navy, Robert F. Scott, set sail for Ross Island, and onwards on foot to explore a vast section of the Antarctic continent. One of Scott's team, a 27-year-old Merchant Navy officer, appointed third lieutenant in charge of holds, stores, provisions and deep-seawater analysis, was called Ernest Shackleton.

The Discovery Expedition carried out extensive scientific research and geographical exploration, finding the Polar Plateau that is home to the South Pole, the axis of the Earth's rotation and the southernmost point on the planet.

4

This 1618 map of Terra Australis Incognita, 'unknown southern land', describes a continent running from New Guinea to South America.

James Clark Ross's ships *Erebus* and *Terror* were warships with extremely strong hulls (built to withstand the recoil of their bomb mortars), and served well in thick ice.

Ernest Henry Shackleton was born in County Kildare, Ireland, on 15 February 1874. His family moved to London when Ernest was ten years old and he was educated at Dulwich College before, as a restless 16-year-old, and in defiance of his father's wishes that he train as a doctor, he joined the Merchant Navy. He spent the best part of a decade at sea before joining Scott's Discovery Expedition.

Just three years after his return in 1904, Shackleton sailed for Antarctica again as the leader of the Nimrod Expedition – formally called the British Antarctic Expedition – an audacious plan which sparked a rivalry with Captain Scott that lasted until Scott's death in Antarctica in 1912.

After spending winter in their base at McMurdo Sound, Ernest and his three companions, Frank Wild, Jameson Adams and Eric Marshall, set off on foot towards the South Pole. Shackleton and his team endured a harrowing 73-day journey south before turning for home, just 97.5 nautical miles short of the South Pole. High on the Antarctic Plateau, they were dangerously low on food and supplies. Shackleton wrote to his wife of his decision to turn home within a hair's breadth of his prize: 'I thought you would prefer a live donkey to a dead lion.'

Shackleton returned, in 1909, to a hero's welcome, a knighthood from King Edward VII, and to the Norwegian explorer Roald Amundsen proclaiming that '[w]hat Nansen is to the North, Shackleton is to the South'. However, the Pole had still not been reached.

Shackleton in his White Star Line uniform, 1890.
Dulwich College in the background is the final resting place of the *James Caird* lifeboat (see page 36).

The race to become the first to reach the South Pole continued, and in August 1910, Captain Scott set sail for Antarctica once more, in command of the Terra Nova Expedition. Unbeknownst to Scott, Amundsen had also set sail from Norway for the far south aboard the *Fram*, leading an expedition with eighteen men and a hundred North Greenland sled dogs.

Scott and his men landed and overwintered at Ross Island, before setting off for the South Pole on foot in the austral spring of 1911, following the exact route pioneered by Shackleton and his men on the Nimrod Expedition. Scott, and his four teammates Edward Wilson, Edgar Evans, Henry Bowers and Lawrence Oates, arrived at the South Pole in January 1912 after ten weeks of travel to find, to their horror, that they had been beaten to it. Roald Amundsen and seven of his crew had already become the first people in history to reach the South Pole, setting foot at the southernmost point on Earth on 14 December 1911. Unlike Scott's men, who were wearing harnesses and man-hauling their own supplies, Amundsen had used dogs and dog sleds with brutal efficiency, starting with fifty-three dogs and finishing with eleven.

Exhausted and demoralized to find to find this ultimate prize snatched from their grasp, Scott and his men turned north and began the return march to the coast, but all five perished before reaching safety. The story of the deaths of Scott and his team became a tragedy that captivated a nation.

With the South Pole attained by Norway, Shackleton decided there was 'but one great main object of Antarctic journeyings' and announced in January 1914 his plan to cross the Antarctic continent, from one coast to another via the Pole, an expedition in which 'every step will be of great scientific importance'.

Amundsen's expedition was meticulously planned. He studied Inuit wilderness survival techniques and designed his own snow goggles, dog harnesses and wooden-soled boots.

In the scale and complexity of its logistics, the Imperial Trans-Antarctic Expedition was the most ambitious expedition ever to set sail for Antarctica. Shackleton's plan required two ships, the *Endurance* and the *Aurora*, four sledging parties and fifty-six men. The expedition's overall budget was estimated to be £80,000 (the equivalent of £6.9 million at the time of writing) and was heavily reliant on the support of commercial sponsors and individual benefactors.

Shackleton's own boat, the *Endurance*, captained by New Zealand sailor Frank Worsley, would head for the Weddell Sea, on the South American side of Antarctica. Upon reaching the coast, the crew were to construct a hut to shelter in for the bitter cold and 24-hour darkness of the coming winter. Shackleton had already overwintered at Cape Royds, on the opposite side of Antarctica during his Nimrod Expedition, and his small wooden hut, as well as Scott's Discovery and Terra Nova huts, still stand to this day.

When the sun rose above the horizon again in the austral spring of 1915, three teams would then set off. Two of the teams would conduct scientific research in Graham Land and Enderby Land, while the third, the Transcontinental Party – led by Shackleton himself – would set out for the Pole, and then on to the Ross Sea on the opposite side of the continent, a total distance of 1,800 miles. The first half of this journey would be over the West Antarctic Ice Sheet, which had never been explored.

The 'MEN WANTED' advert supposedly placed by Shackleton in the *Times* was almost certainly invented for a 1940s book. Shackleton did however write a letter to the newspaper in December 1913, prompting nearly 5,000 replies that were sorted as either 'Mad', Hopeless' or 'Possible'.

MEN WANTED

for hazardous journey, small wages, bitter cold, long mo____ of complete darkness, consta_____, safe return doubtful, ho_____ cognition in case of succes____

Ernest Shacklet_____gton st.

While the *Endurance* sailed for the Weddell Sea, the *Aurora*, under the command of Captain Aeneas Mackintosh, was set to sail – via Sydney and then Hobart – to Antarctica's Ross Sea, and finally to McMurdo Sound, where the team would look for a spot to construct a hut that would serve as their base camp for nearly two years. After landing stores and supplies, and building and then overwintering in a prefabricated wooden hut, the Ross Sea Party's nineteen men would make a series of sledge journeys across the 400-mile-wide Ross Ice Shelf (referred to at the time as The Barrier), positioning a series of supply depots for the Transcontinental Party to collect on the final quarter of their traverse of the continent.

The *Aurora*, built in Dundee in 1876 as a whaler, had already seen Antarctic service as part of the Australian explorer Douglas Mawson's 1911–14 Australasian Antarctic Expedition, and Shackleton bought the ship from Mawson in 1914.

Although the Ross Sea Party's main responsibility was to lay supply depots – and as Sir Ernest's team would be unable to haul sufficient supplies for the entire expedition, their survival would depend entirely on Mackintosh and his men's ability to carry out this mission – the party also had a small scientific team that would carry out research in the Ross Sea region. This fieldwork would include recording meteorological and glaciological observations, tidal recordings and the collection of zoological specimens.

On 8 August 1914, four days after the outbreak of the First World War, and on Winston Churchill's orders as First Lord of the Admiralty, the *Endurance* set sail from Plymouth for Buenos Aires. Shackleton had volunteered, with the agreement of all hands, the services of his ship and his men to support the burgeoning war effort, but was told that the authorities 'desired that the Expedition, which had the full sanction and support of the Scientific and Geographic Societies, should go on'.

The 350-ton, 144-foot *Endurance*, built in 1912 of oak, Norwegian fir and greenheart by the Framnæs shipyard in Norway, had been designed specifically to navigate the semi-frozen ocean at the highest latitudes. Initially named *Polaris*, the ship had three masts and a coal-fired steam-engine, and was capable of a top speed of 10 knots.

At the time of her launch, the ship was arguably the strongest wooden vessel ever built. Her keel was constructed of four pieces of solid oak, with a combined thickness of 85 inches (2.2 m) while the ship's hull was between 30 inches (76 cm) and 18 inches (46 cm) thick, braced with twice as many supporting frames as normal. The bow, designed to ram and split thinner ice floes, was built from timber from a single oak tree, chosen for its shape which followed the line of the shipbuilder's design.

The *Endurance* arrived in Argentina after an uneventful three months at sea. From here the men sailed to the island of South Georgia, where they carried out their final preparations. The island was home to whaling stations during the first half of the twentieth century that fed Europe's vast demand for whale oil, to fuel lamps and produce margarine and soap. South Georgia was the last inhabited land mass before Antarctica.

As well as a complement of twenty-eight men, the *Endurance* was home to sixty-nine dogs, sturdy animals – most were crossbreeds, averaging 45 kg in weight – chosen for their fortitude and purchased from the Hudson Bay Company in Canada. The dogs sailed separately from Liverpool, which allowed the expedition's carpenter, Henry McNish, to oversee the construction of kennels along the port and starboard sides of the ship's deck on its journey to Buenos Aires.

In order to train the dogs for their forthcoming journey, pulling heavy sleds across Antarctica, they were organized into six teams under the command of James McIlroy, Frank Hurley, Alexander Macklin, Tom Crean, George Marston and Frank Wild. If Shackleton and his men were to cross the continent in 120 days, the dogs would have to cover 15 to 20 miles per day, with full loads.

Shackleton also planned to use motorized sleds to cross from the west of Antarctica to the Pole. Captain Scott had tried and failed to use tractors to pull sleds on his Terra Nova Expedition. Amundsen had proved the effectiveness of using dog sleds, but Shackleton believed mechanized sleds would be superior, and employed an expert, Thomas Orde-Lees, to test his redesigned vehicles in Norway. His plan was to use five petrol-powered sleds, three 'aero-motor sleds', driven by a large propeller, and two with caterpillar tracks.

With their preparations complete, the crew of the *Endurance* set sail for Antarctica on 5 December 1914. Their aim was to land at Vahsel Bay, an area discovered by the German explorer Wilhelm Filchner in 1911, where they would overwinter through the 24-hour darkness before attempting their crossing. However, to make landfall, the *Endurance* first had to negotiate the notoriously hostile Weddell Sea. Filchner had had to abandon his own ship, the *Deutschland*, in 1912, after it became trapped in sea ice, so Shackleton was aware of the potential risk that lay ahead.

Avoiding 'growlers', treacherous fragments of ice that float just under the ocean surface, Worsley navigated the *Endurance* past a growing number of icebergs, before the ship encountered pack ice far further north than its crew had hoped. The floating skin of ice that surrounds Antarctica grows and shrinks each year as the seasons change. It usually reaches its maximum extent in midwinter (July) and its minimum in midsummer (December).

Amidst the ice, south of the Antarctic Circle, the crew spotted humpback and finner whales; birds, including petrels, fulmars and white-rumped terns, flew overhead, while the Adélie penguins provided as much amusement for the crew as the ship did for them. The men were able to hunt off the side of the ship, and the seal meat they brought back was a welcome addition to their rations.

Emperor penguin

Adélie penguin

Albatross

Shearwater

Leopard seal

Elephant seal

Humpback whale

Minke whale

In January 1915, the *Endurance* became inextricably caught up in the pack ice of the Weddell Sea. As the sun and the temperature dropped, it became apparent that there was no chance of the ship being freed until the following spring.

Shackleton ordered that the crew dispense with the ship's normal routine, and the vessel became a 'winter station', with all hands on duty during the day and all – except one lone watchman to keep an eye on the dogs and the ice – sleeping at night. The dog kennels were moved from the deck of the ship on to the surrounding ice, and the men shot as many seals as they could, to bolster their supplies of food for the coming weeks of frozen darkness. In addition to their hunting expeditions, Shackleton's crew passed the time by playing games of hockey and football on flat areas of ice near the ship.

The men worked on the ship, creating a living and dining room for officers and scientists that housed the stove they had intended for their shore hut. It soon became known as The Ritz, 'a scene of noisy merriment, in strange contrast with the cold, silent world that lay outside'. Like astronauts visiting a distant planet, they were now at least ten months' travel away from home, with no communication, no chance of rescue and no news of the raging World War that had already claimed millions of lives.

As the Antarctic winter set in, the *Endurance* – held fast by the pack ice – drifted slowly north with the ocean currents and the prevailing southwesterly wind. At such an extreme latitude, summers brought 24-hour daylight, but midwinter this far south meant complete darkness. The men saw the last of the sun on 1 May as it sunk below the horizon shortly before 2 p.m., not to return again until the following spring, in September.

Temperatures regularly fell below −35°C, and while Shackleton did his best to keep his men occupied through training runs (and races) with the dog teams, and more and more games of hockey and football, he feared the drift would carry the ship too far northeast for him to land at Vahsel Bay in the coming spring. The surrounding coastline was largely unmapped, and Shackleton relied on charts and accounts from Wilhelm Filchner's expedition to the Weddell Sea, four years previously, to choose his landing site. 'Can we reach any suitable spot early enough to attempt the overland journey next year?' he wrote. 'Time alone will tell . . . In the meantime, we must wait.'

The ice floe around the *Endurance* started to disintegrate in a storm in early August.

With winter turning to spring, and temperatures slowly rising from the minus thirties to only a few degrees below freezing, the pack ice began to break up. Sightings of 'water sky' – the dark surface of open water in the distance being reflected on the undersides of clouds – gave the men hope that they might be underway again soon, but the remorseless grinding pressure of millions of tons of moving pack ice began to crush their helplessly lodged vessel.

By the third week of October, the *Endurance* had begun taking on water through widening cracks in its hull. McNish, the ship's carpenter, led efforts to keep the leaks in check by nailing strips of wood over cracks in the *Endurance*'s hull and plugging gaps with blankets. Shackleton's concern was clear, and he wrote in his diary that he felt like an intruder in a strange world, 'our lives dependent on the play of grim elementary forces that made a mock of our puny efforts'.

On Wednesday 27 October, the crew finally abandoned the ship that they thought would be taking them home, pitching camp on a nearby ice floe with an uncertain fate ahead. Three weeks later, the crushed and twisted wreckage of the *Endurance* finally slipped beneath the surface of the ice and sank. Shackleton wrote that 'the loss of the ship meant more to us than can ever be put into words'. A year after first reaching the pack ice, they were at an almost identical latitude to that which they had reached with high hopes twelve months previously.

With their ship gone, Shackleton had to take stock of the expedition's situation. The men were camped on the semi-frozen surface of the sea, on a floating ice floe drifting at the mercy of the winds, some 500 miles from the nearest outpost of civilization.

The first makeshift camp on the ice became known as Dump Camp, owing to the amount of unnecessary equipment that was abandoned there as they set off on foot across the ice. Fresh sets of clothing and sleeping bags were issued, tents were pitched and tea brewed before the men set to work reinforcing the sledges that would haul the three lifeboats across the ice.

After a gruelling first day's march through wet, deep snow, Shackleton decided to establish a new camp, called Ocean Camp. Barely a mile and a half from the wreck of the *Endurance*, this was to become their home for almost two months. Even with twenty-first-century clothing and equipment, life under canvas in Antarctica can be extremely challenging, and the difficulties of the men's day-to-day existence are hard to imagine.

Despite their dire situation, the men remained for the most part optimistic. Food was vital both to survival and morale, and they soon set to work building a makeshift galley for the cook out of sails and tarpaulins. Once that was complete, they used pieces of planking from *Endurance*'s deck to build a lookout, with a mast that flew the king's flag.

Living conditions on the floating pack ice continued to deteriorate as the days passed. The men suffered perpetually wet feet, and condensation froze on the inside of their tents at night, showering them with hoar frost when they stirred the next morning. Moving around on the ice, they frequently fell through thin crusts of snow into the water beneath.

The cook, Charles Green, worked perpetually at his improvised stove. Built from parts foraged from the *Endurance*'s engine room and an oil drum, with a biscuit-tin chimney, it burned seal blubber, which gave the food a revolting flavour. Shackleton was keen to preserve his specially made, lightweight sledging rations, so the team began instead to eat the dog food, a form of pemmican (a mixture of oats and animal fat), while the surviving dogs ate seal meat.

Flour and sugar, salvaged from the ship, were precious luxuries, and seal and penguin meat, either boiled or fried over the stove, began to make up almost the entirety of the men's diet as supplies dwindled. The men hunted for seal every day, both for food and for blubber to keep the stove going. Meals were often watered down into 'hoosh' – a stew or thick soup – and were serious occasions, with little conversation and with bowls scraped spotlessly clean. To avoid any favouritism when meals were served, one of the men was picked at each mealtime and asked to close his eyes and call the names of his teammates at random when asked 'Whose?' by the cook.

The fact that we have such a vivid record of the Endurance Expedition is due to the diligence of Shackleton and his men as diarists, and in no small part to the work of Frank Hurley, the expedition's photographer. This was not Hurley's first trip to Antarctica: the 29-year-old Australian had already accompanied Douglas Mawson's expedition in 1911, and made a film of their journey called *Home of the Blizzard*.

Hurley used the recently patented Paget process to produce colour photographs of the Endurance Expedition, and taking each shot was a painstaking operation that required two glass plates. He also shot motion footage in order to make a film on their return.

When the *Endurance* began to sink, Hurley spent three days on the adjacent ice, capturing the ill-fated ship in her final throes. He went on board to salvage his film canisters from the wreck, diving into the icy water in the ships bowels to retrieve the tins of negatives. A week later, Hurley was given the heart-breaking task of destroying 400 of his glass photographic plates to reduce the weight of the equipment the men would have to carry on their arduous trek towards salvation. The 120 plates that survived, along with the black-and-white photographs from a small pocket camera that Hurley used on Elephant Island, make up the only visual record of one of the most remarkable journeys in history.

The men treated 22 December 1915 as Christmas Day. As the temperatures rose and the ice around the camp began to break up, Shackleton decided to attempt the march west once more, with the aim of finding open water to put to sea in *Endurance*'s three lifeboats, and eventually rescuing his men. The remaining stock of luxuries was turned into a last feast in order to minimize the weight that needed to be dragged across the floes.

After a seven-day march, hauling the lifeboats behind them, the men were worn out. They had covered just 7.5 miles, and they knew the nearest land was still 300 miles away. Shackleton had little option but to establish their third home on the ice – Patience Camp.

Shackleton's sights were at first set on reaching Paulet Island, where he knew there was a hut and stores, which he himself had ordered to be sent there to rescue the Swedish explorer Otto Nordenskjöld's expedition in 1904. However, these hopes soon faded as the current carried the men east, towards Elephant Island.

On 9 April 1916, having lived on the floating pack ice for almost six months and drifting inexorably north towards the open sea, the expedition was finally forced into the boats – and on to the unfathomed ocean – as the floes disintegrated.

The voyage to Elephant Island lasted five days. Sailing through the night, at the mercy of the winds, the men in the three lifeboats faced increasingly desperate conditions. They could not sleep because of the severe cold (they recorded −29°C), and desperate thirst and dehydration struck every one of them as the sea spray tantalized their swollen mouths. Killer whales were another constant source of anxiety. When one of the men on the *Stancomb Wills* (the lifeboats were named after Shackleton's three most generous sponsors) called out that he could do with some dry mittens, Shackleton smiled and later wrote in his diary that 'he might as well have asked for the moon'. Despite horrendous conditions and an uncertain heading, the men maintained their faith in Shackleton's leadership.

As they made landfall on Elephant Island and the stores were unloaded, Shackleton noticed that the men were reeling about the beach, laughing and picking up handfuls of pebbles. This was the first time they had set foot on solid ground in nearly 500 days.

They set up camp on a precarious spit of beach, surrounded by tall cliffs and impenetrable glaciers, and immediately began killing seals and penguins for food. Hundreds of miles from the nearest shipping routes, on an inhospitable island with no hope of being rescued, Shackleton remained stoic and upbeat as he realized another stage of the homeward journey had been achieved.

After an assessment of their situation, Shackleton decided that another boat journey in search of relief was necessary. South Georgia lay 800 miles away, but was home to whalers – experienced in sailing the Southern Ocean – who could help launch a rescue mission.

A crew of six was chosen, and the carpenter, 'Chippy' McNish, set about modifying the *James Caird* for a long journey on the high seas. Using the sled runners and tent canvas, McNish, Timothy McCarthy and Alfred Cheetham crafted a flimsy deck for the small vessel, as well as strengthening the keel with the scavenged mast of the *Stancomb Wills*.

On 24 April 1916, as the sun began to sink lower in the sky and the winter crept closer, Shackleton and his crew put to sea on the Sub-Antarctic Ocean with supplies for four weeks. If they did not make it to South Georgia within a month, they stood no chance of saving the shore party who stayed behind, camping under the upturned hulls of the *Dudley Docker* and the *Stancomb Wills*.

Of the sixteen days that followed, Shackleton wrote: 'We fought the seas and the winds and at the same time had a daily struggle to keep ourselves alive.' On four-hour shifts, three men took what rest they could in wet sleeping bags, while the remaining crew battled the forces of Nature at their most severe.

Worsley navigated northeast across the fearsome ocean using dead reckoning – calculating the boat's position using estimated speed and distance covered – and, when he could see them through the cloud and spray, by the position of the stars.

A page of writing can barely do justice to the perils these six men faced on their ocean voyage. That they survived the journey at all is testament to their sheer strength of will.

The men had loaded the *James Caird* with more than a ton of ballast before leaving Elephant Island, consisting of sand-filled bags made from blankets, large boulders from the island's beach, and 250 lbs of ice, to provide drinking water. At sea, they moved the boulders constantly to trim the boat, and found that as a result there was scarcely room to sleep without being curled around a rock, and only room to move below deck on all fours. The space underneath the boat's flimsy roof was constantly wet, and the team's reindeer-skin sleeping bags began to moult due to the moisture, losing their insulation. Cramped in their narrow quarters, the men were continually soaked by salt spray and spent much of their time baling. Shackleton described the wind as 'nearly always' gale-force, with waves taller than he had ever seen in twenty-six years at sea, so high that their small boat's sails flapped idly in the deep troughs between the giant swells. When, after two weeks at sea, the cliffs of South Georgia came into sight, they were aching, weak, frostbitten, tormented by thirst and debilitated by dehydration and exhaustion.

A fearsome storm kept the *James Caird* at sea for another two nights. The swell threatened to drown the little boat, which was in constant danger of being thrown against the rocks or of being wrecked on the nearby Annenkov Island. On 10 May, the wind eased slightly and Shackleton decided that they must attempt a landing, as the weaker members of his crew might not survive another day at sea. After several attempts, they landed at Cave Cove, near the entrance to King Haakon Bay. This was on the uninhabited south side of the island – the whaling stations that promised rescue were on the north.

Rather than risk putting out to sea again to reach Stromness, the manned whaling station on the north coast of South Georgia, a boat journey of more than 100 miles, Shackleton decided to attempt to cross the island on foot, a journey of 32 miles over uncharted terrain.

After a few days' rest to recover from their sea voyage, Shackleton, Captain Worsley and Second Officer Tom Crean set off at 2 a.m. on Friday 18 May. The men had no map and had to improvise a route across South Georgia's jagged mountain ranges and heavily crevassed glaciers, at times reaching an altitude of 4,500 feet – higher than Ben Nevis.

At one point, after walking for twenty-seven hours without taking more than a few minutes' rest, the three men lay down in the lee of a large rock. Crean and Worsley fell asleep immediately, but Shackleton forced himself to stay awake, and woke his two companions after five minutes, telling them they had slept for half an hour.

At 7 a.m. on Saturday 20 May the men heard a steam whistle summoning the whalers to work, and started their descent to Fortuna Bay. At 1.30 p.m. they climbed a final ridge and spotted the people, boats, sheds and factories of Stromness whaling station for the first time. They had travelled continuously for thirty-six hours, and were on the verge of exhaustion, their faces blackened from exposure, frost injury and soot from their blubber stove. Before making their way down a precarious waterfall to safety, Shackleton noted, he and his two travelling companions paused to shake hands, a gesture they had shared on only four occasions during the entire expedition.

As he, Worsley and Crean walked the final few paces to the buildings at Stromness, Shackleton reflected that, despite entering the Antarctic Circle a year and a half previously with high hopes and a well-stocked ship full of tons of provisions and equipment, the only possessions the men now shared were an ice axe, a small stove and their logbook. They had been wearing the same clothes for nearly twelve months, and were bearded, frostbitten, emaciated and unwashed. The first people they encountered – two small boys and one of the workers at the whaling station – ran away from them without exchanging a word, startled by their appearance. They walked through the station to the wharf and the house of the manager, Mr Sorlle, who didn't recognize Shackleton. Sir Ernest's first two questions were 'Don't you recognize me?' and 'When was the war over?'

The men were given baths, food and clean clothes, and that evening, a motorboat was despatched with Worsley to King Haakon Bay to rescue the three men that remained there and to collect the *James Caird*. When the boat arrived, neither McCarthy, McNish nor John Vincent, who had been sheltering beneath the upturned hull of the *Endurance*'s lifeboat, recognized Worsley, their companion of more than eighteen months, who was now clean-shaven and in freshly laundered clothes.

As the austral winter descended and the thickening pack ice began to imprison the men on Elephant Island once again, Shackleton worked tirelessly to rescue the remainder of his crew. Over the course of the next few months, Sir Ernest made four separate bids to reach his men, but he was constantly beaten back by adverse weather and ice conditions. It was not until August 1916, on his fourth attempt and in a small steamer loaned to him by the Chilean government, the *Yelcho*, that Shackleton neared the island and the shore party's camp finally came into view.

Worsley was the first to spot the snow-covered shelter, and the men ashore spotted them at the same time and began waving from the beach. Within an hour, every man had been rescued and was aboard, and the small boat steamed north again at high speed to avoid the drifting floes. The *Yelcho* had a thin, fragile steel hull, and Shackleton had promised its owners that it would not touch the ice.

The twenty-two men on Elephant Island had survived, thanks largely to the resourcefulness and leadership of Shackleton's second-in-command, Frank Wild. When the *Yelcho* arrived, they had only four days of food left. They were also packed and ready to leave, as Wild had been insisting every morning for weeks that 'the Boss' would be rescuing them that day, and that the men should roll up their sleeping bags and pack their belongings ready for the boat.

While all the Endurance's crew were saved, unfortunately the same was not true of Shackleton's Ross Sea Party. In May 1915, shortly after arriving at Cape Evans, the Aurora was ripped away from its anchor during a storm, and drifted away in the night, leaving ten men cut off in Antarctica for almost two years with hardly any of the supplies they had intended to offload from their ship. The Aurora drifted with its crew for nine months, trapped in the sea ice, before eventually limping into port in New Zealand for repairs on its broken rudder.

With no knowledge of Shackleton's predicament, the men assumed that laying the chain of supply depots would be vital to the survival of the team that would be approaching from the other side of the continent, and they started scavenging supplies from Captain Scott's nearby Terra Nova hut, abandoned three years previously.

Woefully ill-equipped, wearing clothes made from an old canvas tent abandoned by Scott and boots fashioned from old reindeer-skin sleeping bags, the men of the Ross Sea Party moved nearly four tons of supplies from Cape Evans to Hut Point, twelve miles away, before embarking on the journey to position depots. Six of the men went on to make continuous sled journeys across McMurdo Sound and the Ross Ice Shelf for seven months. On their return journey to Ross Island, Rev. Arnold Spencer-Smith collapsed with exhaustion and died a few days later. Upon reaching the coast, the men sheltered from a storm at Scott's near-empty Discovery hut. Their rations were no more, and they survived for days on seal meat alone before two of the team, Captain Mackintosh and Victor Hayward, decided to set out for Cape Evans on foot across the sea ice.

They were never seen again.

Shackleton sailed to New Zealand in late 1916, to oversee the rescue of the Ross Sea Party. By this stage, the finances of the Endurance Expedition were in a perilous position, and the governments of Australia, New Zealand and Great Britain agreed to fund the rescue mission, insisting on their joint committee having control of the relief expedition. Shackleton and the *Aurora* – now under the command of Captain John Davis – set sail for McMurdo Sound in December 1916.

The *Aurora* reached the hut at Cape Evans on 10 January, and the seven survivors of the shore party (the three remaining depot-layers had managed to struggle back across thick sea ice the previous July) were astonished to see Shackleton approaching them by boat, realizing for the first time that their two years of toil had been in vain. The *Aurora* returned to New Zealand in February, and Sir Ernest finally made it home to the United Kingdom in May 1917, three years after first setting sail on the *Endurance*.

He returned amidst the carnage of the First World War, and found that the popular conception of heroism had changed after the horrors of the trenches. Against the hellish backdrop of Ypres and the Somme, his tales of 'white warfare' in the far south seemed of little importance to the public. Most of his men went straight to the front lines, some finding Arctic warfare roles in Russia and the North Sea. Having come unscathed through the dangers of the Antarctic, the crew of the Endurance Expedition took their places in the wider field of battle.

Sir Ernest Shackleton's Endurance Expedition fell a long way short of achieving its planned crossing of Antarctica. Indeed, more than a century later, a surface journey from the Weddell Sea to the South Pole, then descending the Beardmore Glacier to the Ross Ice Shelf and Ross Island has never been made. Yet Shackleton succeeded in carrying out a rescue journey that few others could envisage, and that fewer still could have managed.

Despite public indifference to his homecoming in 1917, this story of endeavour, of survival in the harshest conditions and of sheer grit and determination in the face of the steepest odds has become legendary. Shackleton's rescue of almost his entire crew remains unparalleled, both as a tale of Edwardian derring-do and as a paragon of leadership.

Four years later, in September 1921, Shackleton set sail once more for Antarctica aboard the Quest, as commander of the British Oceanographical and Sub-Antarctic Expedition. On 5 January 1922, Shackleton suffered a fatal heart attack at sea. He was forty-seven when he died, and was buried on South Georgia, by the small chapel at Grytviken, where his body remains to this day.

Shackleton's legacy lives on, with his story serving as an example of bravery, tenacity and decision-making under pressure that is cited at the Harvard Business School and celebrated in books, films, television shows and memorials, including a statue outside the Royal Geographical Society in London. Launched in 1995, the RRS *Ernest Shackleton* continues to support British scientific bases in Antarctica to this day.

Amundsen said of Sir Ernest: 'No man fails who sets an example of high courage, of unbroken resolution, of unshrinking endurance.' Fittingly, Shackleton's family motto reads '*Fortitudine vincimus*' – 'By endurance we conquer.'

Further Reading

Sir Ernest Shackleton *South: The Endurance Expedition* (Penguin Classics, 2015)

Frank Hurley *South with Endurance – Shackleton's Antarctic Expedition 1914–1917: The Photographs of Frank Hurley* (Bloomsbury, 2001)

Shackleton loved poetry, and his gravestone is inscribed with the words 'I hold . . . that a man should strive to the uttermost for his life's set prize', taken from 'The Statue and the Bust'.
Robert Browning *Selected Poems* (Penguin Classics, 2000)

Apsley Cherry-Garrard *The Worst Journey in the World* (Vintage Classics, 2010)

The Scott Polar Research Institute (SPRI) in Cambridge has a permanent exhibition that covers Shackleton's life and career – **www.spri.cam.ac.uk**

Between October 2013 and February 2014, my teammate Tarka l'Herpiniere and I made a 1,801-mile return journey to the South Pole on foot, the first ever completion of the journey that Shackleton attempted on his Nimrod Expedition, and that Captain Scott died attempting in 1912 – **scottexpedition.com**